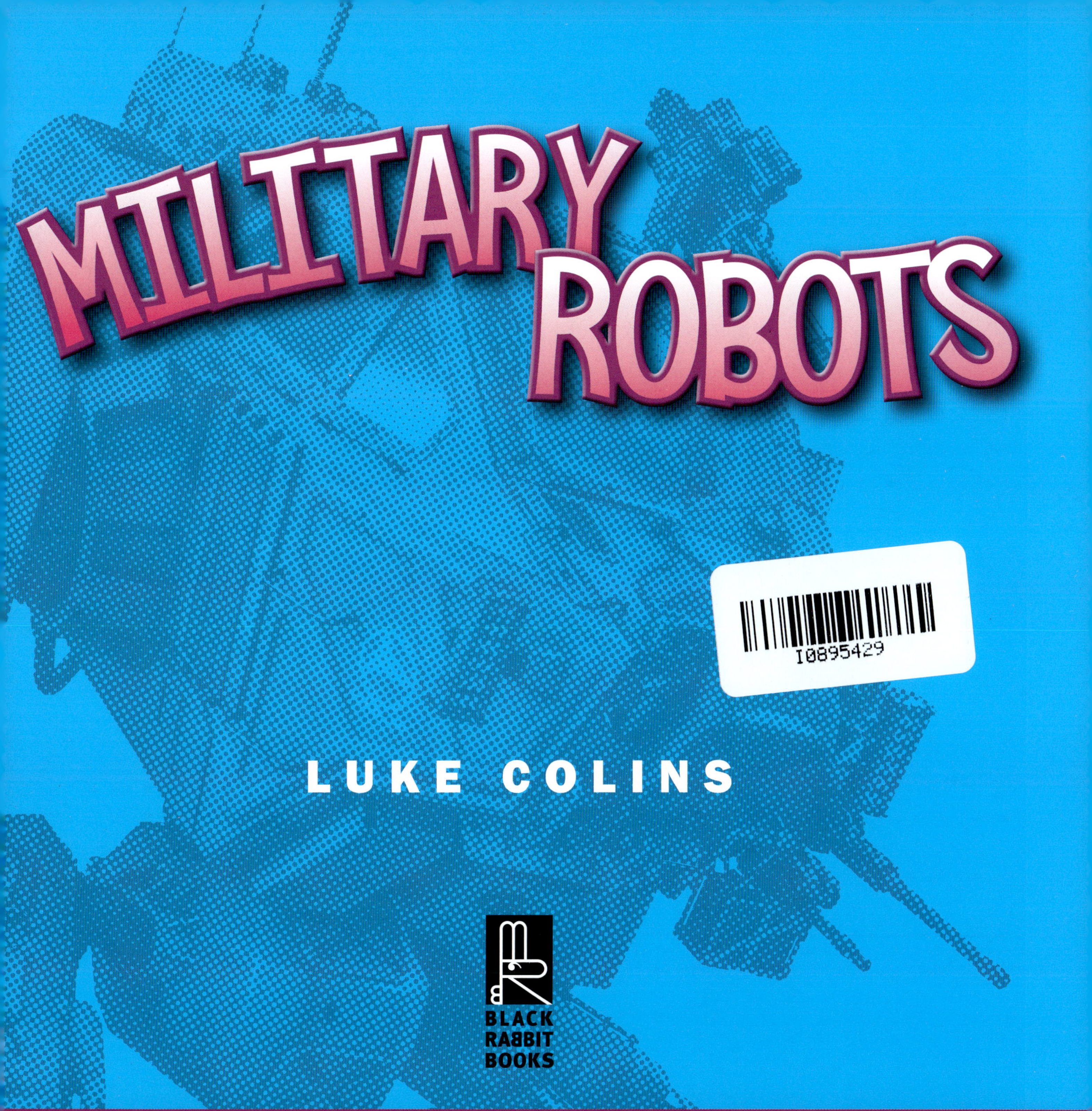

MILITARY ROBOTS

LUKE COLINS

BLACK RABBIT BOOKS

Bolt Jr. is published by Black Rabbit Books
P.O. Box 3263, Mankato, Minnesota, 56002.
www.blackrabbitbooks.com

Grant Gould, designer; Omay Ayres, photo researcher

Names: Colins, Luke, author.
Title: Military robots / by Luke Colins.
Description: Mankato, Minnesota : Black Rabbit Books, [2020] | Series: Bolt Jr. World of robots | Includes bibliographical references and index. | Audience: Age 6-8. | Audience: Grades K-3. | Identifiers: LCCN 2019003764 (print) | LCCN 2019004875 (ebook) | ISBN 9781623101718 (e-book) | ISBN 9781623101657 (library binding) | ISBN 9781644661093 (paperback)
Subjects: LCSH: Military robots—Juvenile literature.
Classification: LCC UG450 (ebook) | LCC UG450 .C54 2020 (print) | DDC 623—dc23
LC record available at https://lccn.loc.gov/2019003764

Printed in the United States. 5/19

Image Credits

ai.stanford.edu: Ruixiang Zhang, 16–17; Alamy: Aflo Co. Ltd., 18–19 (bot); Ivan Mollov, 18 (bkgd); Stocktrek Images, Inc., 5; commons.wikimedia.org: Jjamwal, 8–9; defenceupdate.in: Indian Defence Update, 6–7; phys.org: North Rhine-Westphalia State Office of Criminal Investigation, 21; robots.ieee.org: Endeavor Robotics, 22–23; Shutterstock: aapsky, 12 (drone); DM7, 1; Efman, 13; EmiliaUngur, 12 (jet); FabianGame, 14 (bkgd); Gorodenkoff, 10–11; Kletr, 10; Lukas Davidziuk, 20–21; Martin Nezval, 3, 24; Piotr Debowski, Cover; Steve Oehlenschlager, 7; Warut Chinsai, 4

Contents

CHAPTER 1

Helpful Bots

A **military** truck travels on a road. Suddenly, the driver spots a **bomb**! Soldiers pull a robot from the truck. The bot rolls toward the bomb. The bot shuts the bomb down.

military: relating to soldiers, an army, or war

bomb: a weapon that explodes

COMPARING WINGSPANS

MQ-9 Reaper flying robot
66 feet
(20 meters)

Staying Safe

Military bots have many jobs. Some stop bombs. Others fly and shoot enemies. The bots do dangerous work. Soldiers can then stay safer.

wandering albatross
about 11 feet (3 m)

PARTS OF A Bomb Bot

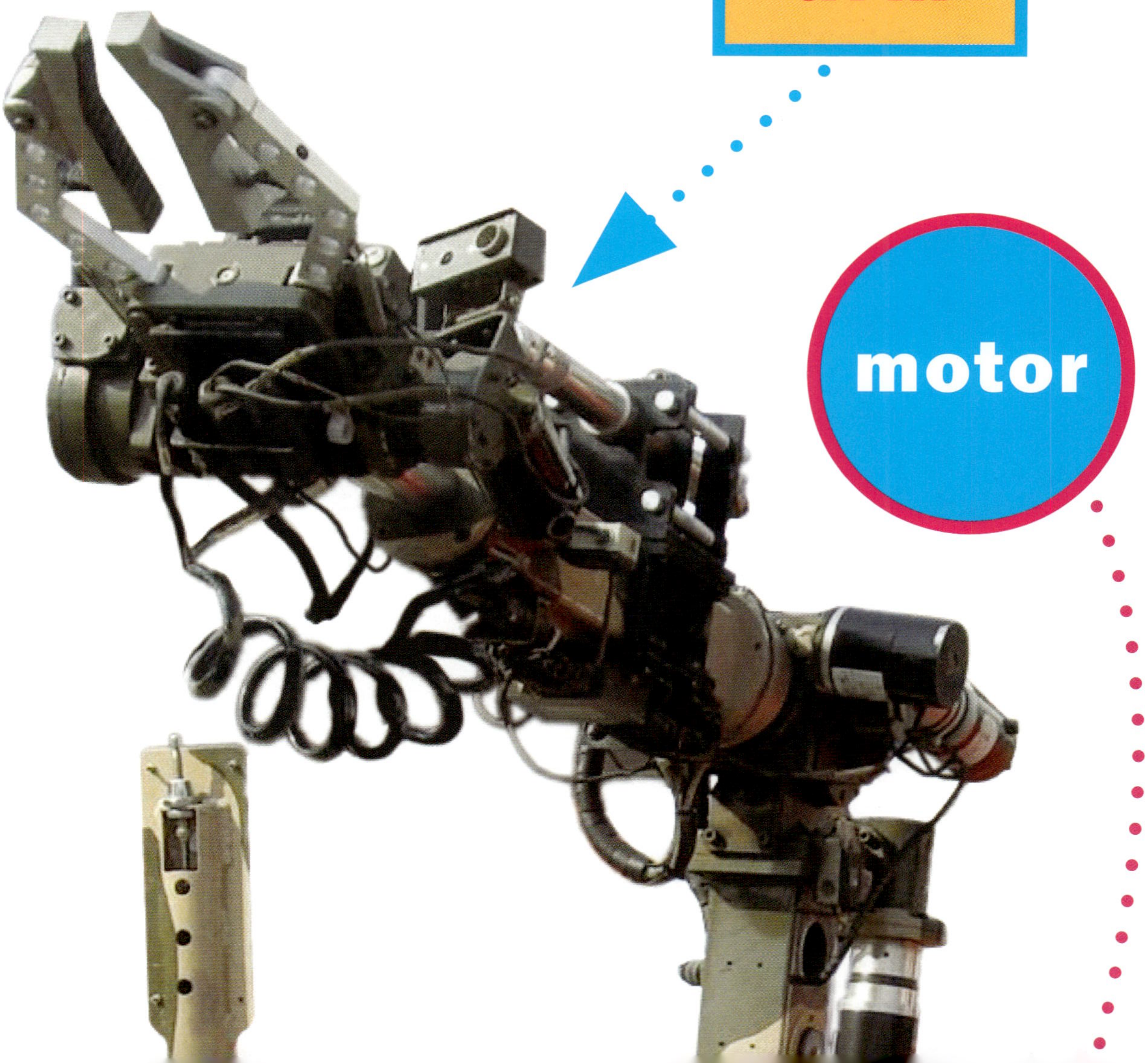

cameras
wheels

CHAPTER 2

Flying Bots

Flying bots are called drones. People use **remote controls** to tell them where to go. These bots take pictures of secret places. Some can shoot weapons.

remote control: a device for controlling something from a distance

FACT
Some drones drop bombs.

Hard to See

Flying bots are smaller than jets. People miss them in the sky. They can't see them on **radar** either.

radar: a device that finds the location and speed of a moving object

Drones with Weapons

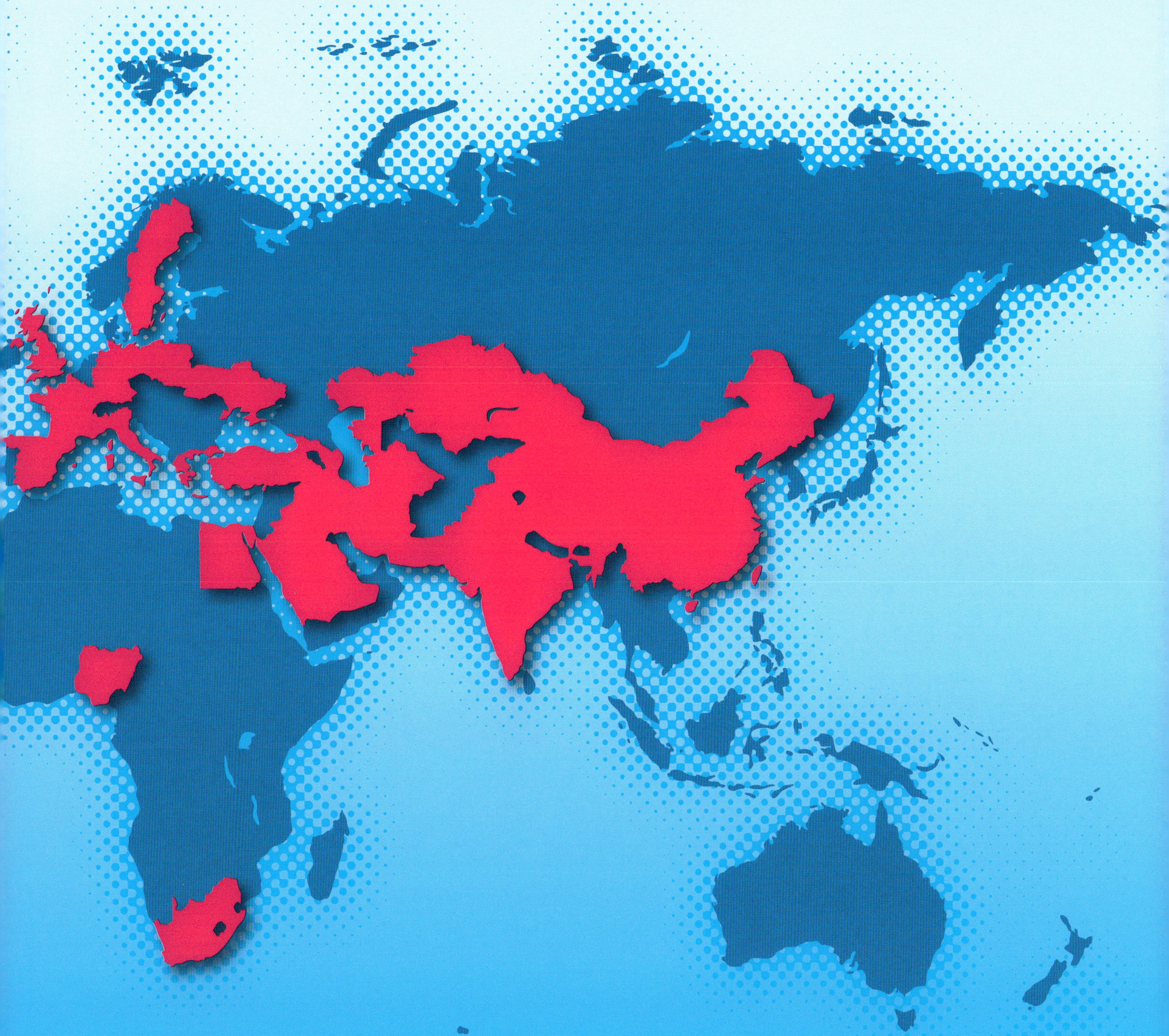

CHAPTER 3

Bomb Bots

Militaries use bomb bots too. The bots roll over rough land. Some even climb stairs. Soldiers control the bots' arms. They use the arms to cut bomb wires.

FACT
One bot can move cars.

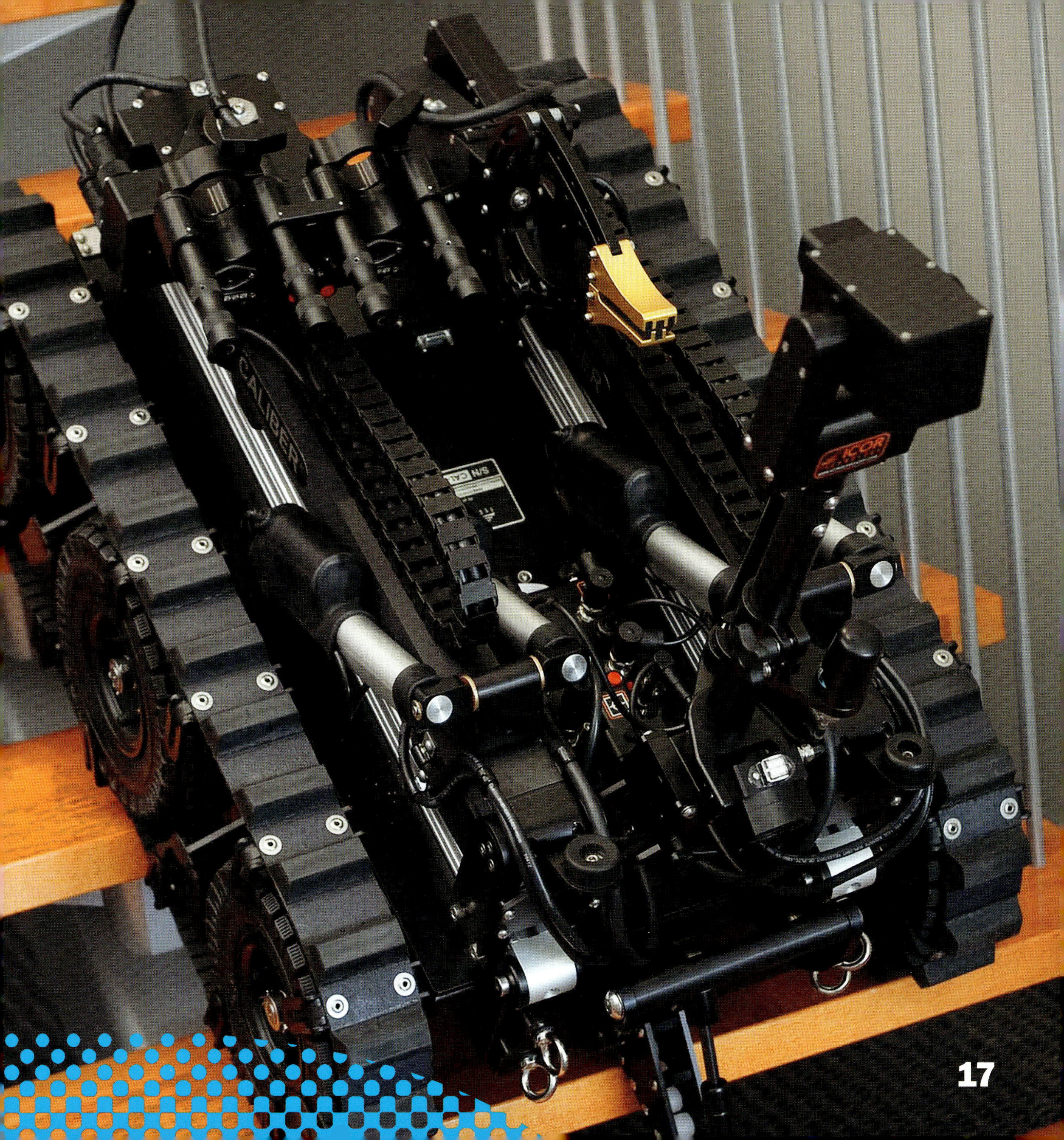
CALIBER
ICOR

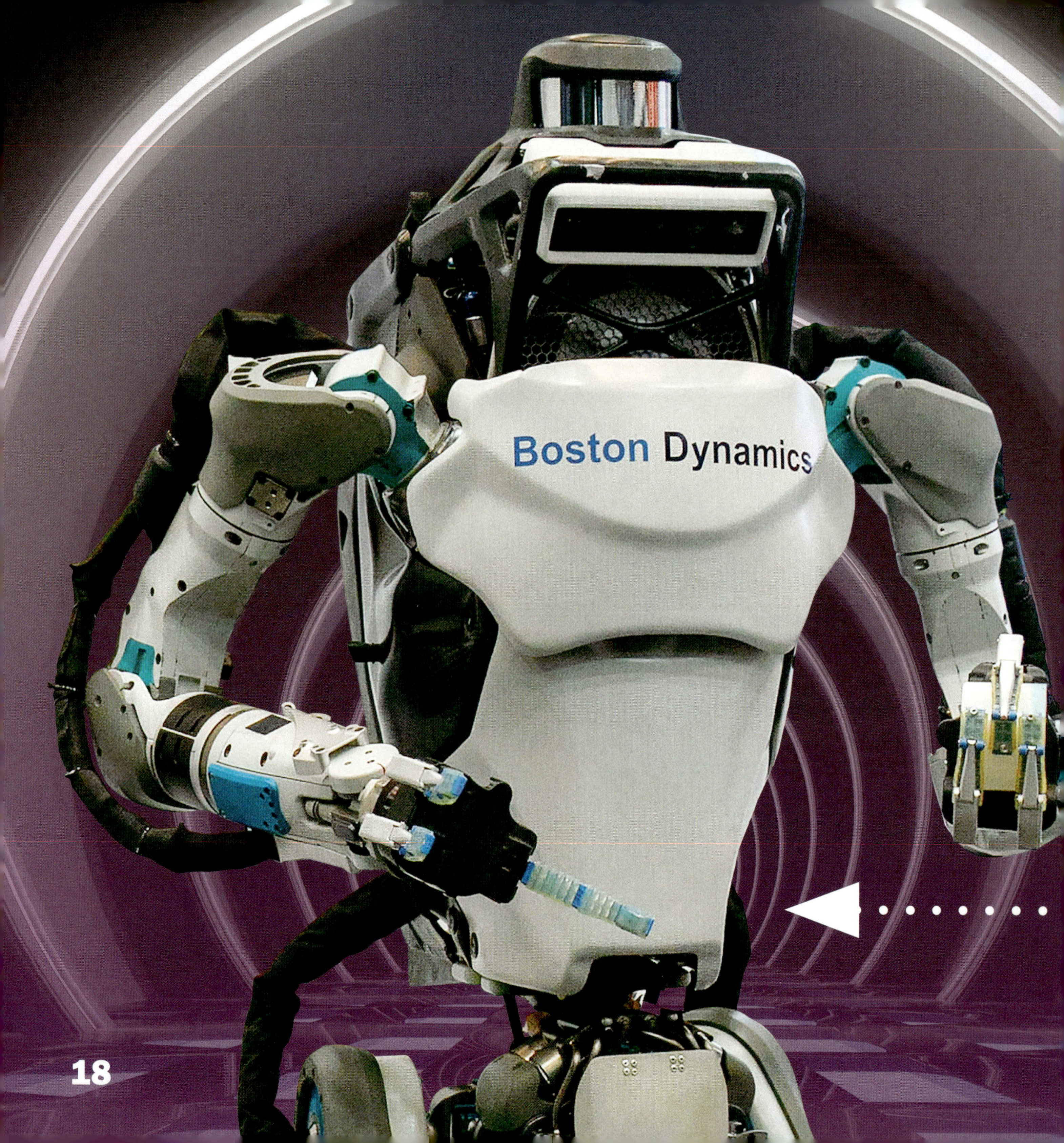
Boston Dynamics

The Future

Robots will continue to help soldiers. Scientists are making new bots. One is human shaped. It uses tools people use. Maybe someday bots will fight in place of people.

The Atlas Robot's Height

5.75 feet
(1.75 m)

Bonus Facts

Some bomb bots have guns.

One flying bot goes **300 miles** (483 kilometers) per hour.

The first military bot was a boat.

One bot uses X-ray to find bombs.

X-ray: rays that can pass through objects and make it possible to see inside things

READ MORE/WEBSITES

Kelly, John. *Fixer the Robot.* London: Faber & Faber, 2018.

Larson, Kirsten W. *Military Robots.* Robotics in Our World. Mankato, MN: Amicus High Interest/Amicus Ink, 2018.

Noll, Elizabeth. *Military Robots.* World of Robots. Minneapolis: Bellwether Media, 2018.

Robotics
kidsahead.com/subjects/1-robotics

Robotics: Facts
idahoptv.org/sciencetrek/topics/robots/facts.cfm

Robots for Kids
www.sciencekids.co.nz/robots.html

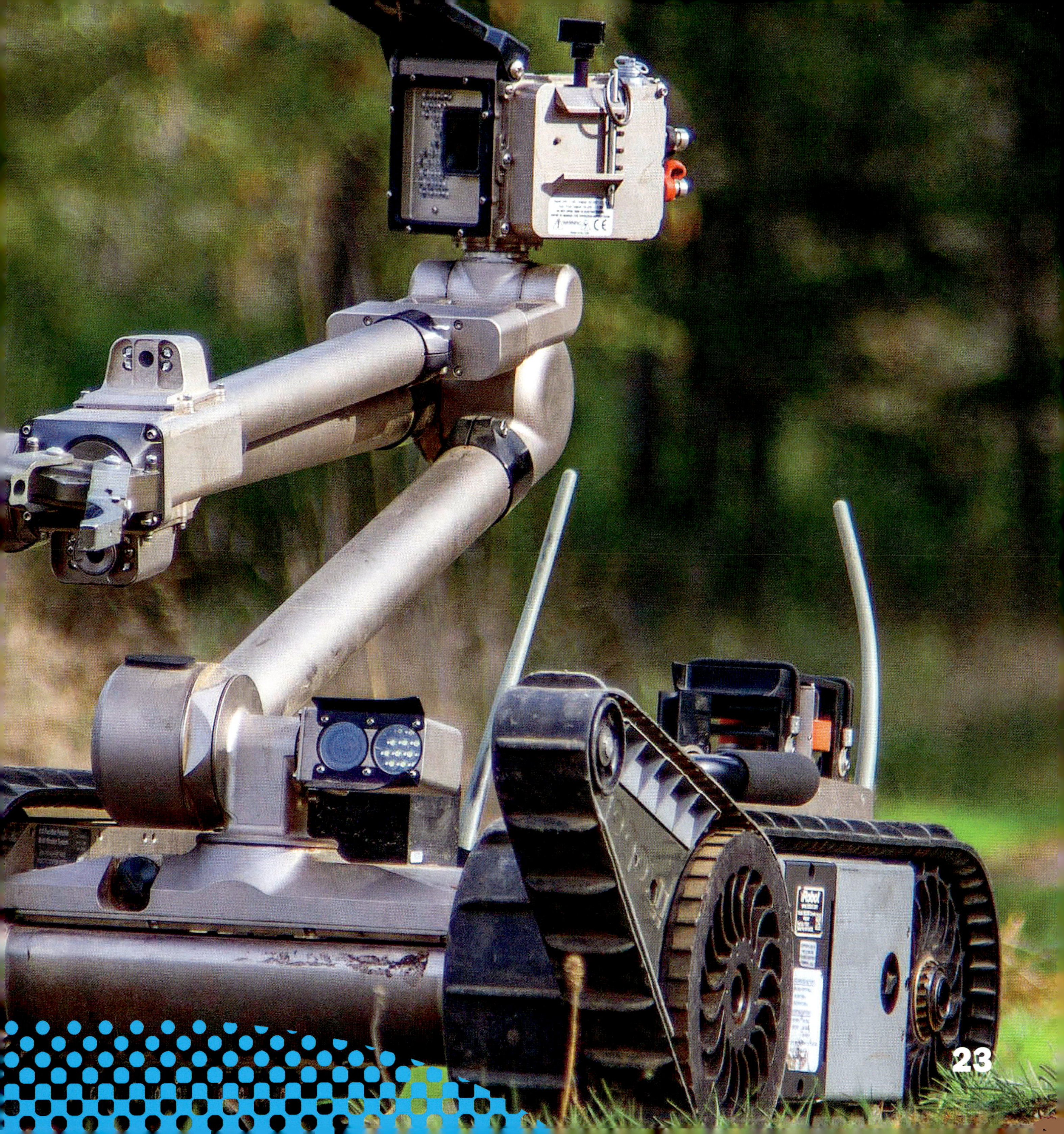

GLOSSARY

bomb (BAHM)—a weapon that explodes

military (MIL-uh-tahr-ee)—relating to soldiers, an army, or war

radar (RAY-dar)—a device that finds the location and speed of a moving object

remote control (ree-MOT kun-TROL)—a device for controlling something from a distance

X-ray (EKS-rey)—rays that can pass through objects and make it possible to see inside

INDEX